空手道
Karate
Made Simple

1 Etiquette, Equipment, and the *Dojo*

Maiko Nakashima
with the Japan Karate Federation

Kneeling in *seiza*

The Oliver Press, Inc.
Minneapolis

INTRODUCTION

Karate-do is a Japanese *budo*, or martial art. It originated on the Japanese island of Okinawa and spread to the rest of Japan. *Budo* is a part of Japanese culture that is based on traditional combat skills. Like all forms of martial arts, the goal of karate is not just to defeat your opponent; it is also to discipline heart, mind, and body through practice and respect for one's opponents.

Karate-do, or the "way of karate," is now known around the world as "karate." In 2010, the World Karate Federation (WKF) had members in 187 countries, and estimates that around 50 million people study karate. Every two years, there is an international tournament, the World Karate Championships, in which athletes gather from all over the world to compete.

By reading this book, you will be able to answer these questions:

- **How is a *rei* performed?**
- **What is a *tatami* in karate?**
- **How does one properly wear and fold a karate *gi*?**

Recently, there has been a movement in Japan to place more importance on traditional Japanese culture, including karate. Starting in 2012, all middle-school students were required to take a *budo* class. Imagine being required to take karate as a gym class!

This series is divided into four books that will introduce you to karate in an easy-to-understand way.

In this series, you will learn how this martial art spread from a small island to become a worldwide phenomenon.

CONTENTS

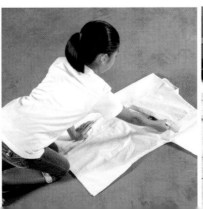

What is *Rei*?

In karate, bowing is more than just a physical action. It is known as rei.

"Begins with *rei* and ends with *rei*."

Karate students always bow upon entering the *dojo*, or training floor, and also when leaving.

Although it is called bowing, *rei* is not just any bow. When you bow, you are giving respect, thanks, and honor to the *sensei* (teacher) who has given you guidance, and to the people with whom you have trained, competed, or sparred.

In other words, what we call *rei* is not just the action of bowing, but also an expression of gratitude, respect, and honor. Often it is said that karate training "begins with *rei* and ends with *rei*." In many ways, *rei* represents the whole philosophy behind karate.

Rei holds this significance not only in karate, but also in judo, kendo, and other Japanese martial arts. It could be said that the philosophy of *rei* is a central characteristic of these martial arts.

Bowing to the altar in front of the *dojo*

Etiquette of *rei*

In karate, if you have respect and compassion for your opponent, this will carry over into your dress, attitude, and speech.

For that reason, if your bow is sloppy and your speech is not polite during practice, then you may be disciplined. Consequently, it is important to perform *rei* properly.

Karate has its own etiquette (rules of behavior) to follow. If you start studying karate, the first thing you will learn is the etiquette of *rei*. Etiquette may vary slightly from school to school.

Rei (bow) and *setsu* (principle)

In karate, *reisetsu* (etiquette, code of conduct) is often used alongside *rei*.

Setsu is distinguishing between what is right and wrong, or holding to a moral code. *Rei* and *setsu* are both important concepts in karate.

These students are demonstrating properly respectful bows.

How to Perform *Rei*

This chapter teaches how to bow correctly. Bowing properly is a way to show respect.

 ## Standing and sitting bow

There are two forms of *rei*. The *ritsurei* is performed while standing. *Zarei* is performed while sitting.

You must start in the correct standing or sitting position to do these bows properly.

Standing bow (*ritsurei*)

1 Align heels with your feet facing outward. Stand up straight. Put your hands on your thighs with your elbows slightly bent.

2 While keeping your spine straight, bend down. Pause and return to the original stance.

Chin down.

Look ahead.

Keep spine straight and stick out chest.

Straighten fingers and place them on the side of body.

Point toes outward so that there is a space about the size of a fist between them.

Look down but slightly forward. Chin up as if face were upright.

Keep knees straight.

Keep spine straight.

Keep hands touching the side of body.

UNACCEPTABLE BOW

Head is too low. Spine is bent.

Hands are in front.

Sitting bow (*zarei*)

1 Keeping spine straight, place both hands with fingers closed on thighs. (See next page for how to kneel properly.)

— Chin down.

Straighten spine and stick out chest.

Square your elbows.

Sit on heels and straighten upper body.

There should a space about the size of a fist between your knees.

2 Keep spine straight and bend upper body. Place left, then right, hand on the floor.

Look straight ahead.

Fingertips point slightly inward, creating a triangle.

3 Tilt your upper body down with elbows bent. Look down at your hands.

Don't hunch your back.

Look at the floor between your hands.

UNACCEPTABLE BOW

The bottom part of the body is raised.

The head is too low.

How to Perform *Seiza*

The traditional way to start or end karate practice is with seiza, *which is a kneeling position. Let's look at the proper way to sit, kneel, and stand.*

 ## Correct way of *seiza*

The body rests on the heels; both hands are on the thighs. When you first start sitting in this position, you may find that your legs start to go numb after a short time. With practice, you will be able to sit in this position longer.

Meditation

In many *dojo*, practice begins and ends with meditating in the *seiza* position. Meditation is closing your eyes and gathering your thoughts. You may be mentally preparing for practice or thinking over what you did during practice that day.

Overlap your big toes.

Meditating while kneeling

Square your chest so that it faces forward.

Place your legs naturally; rest your bottom on your heels.

Hands should be placed with the fingertips on the upper part of the thigh.

Knees should be about one fist width apart.

How to sit and stand

To go from standing to *seiza*, first lower your left knee and then your right. When you stand up, start with your right leg. It is important to keep your back straight throughout the process.

How to sit

1 From the standing position (p.6), slide the left leg straight back and kneel down on the left knee.

Keep the toes bent and directly under the heel.

Right hand rests on the right thigh with the left hand on the side.

2 Kneel down with the right leg.

Keep toes flexed.

Hands on upper thighs.

Why are the toes flexed?

When kneeling, the toes are flexed with the ankle bent. This allows you to be ready to spring into action.

3 Slide the tops of your feet down to the floor and overlap big toes. Sit on your calves.

Knees should be about one fist width apart.

How to stand

1 Start from *seiza* and raise your upper body. Bring your ankles to a 90° angle and flex your toes.

Hands on thighs.

2 Raise the right leg with the left still on the ground.

Keep left toes flexed.

3 Stand up. Heels should be touching.

The *Gi*

Karate students typically wear a uniform, or gi. The gi is worn during sparring (kumite) and when demonstrating forms (kata).

 ## Two ways to wear a *gi*

The *gi* is worn differently for *kata*, which are predetermined sets of movements, and *kumite*, which is free sparring.

The *gi* is worn more snugly for doing *kata*. This style of dress presents a more formal appearance. It is also easier to hear the canvas "snap" when doing a punch or kick. The sound indicates the strength of the technique.

When doing *kumite*, the *gi* is worn more loosely to allow for free movement.

Even though there is a different looseness, where the hems of your pants, jacket, and sleeves should fall on your body is the same. To see the difference in how the *gi* is worn, see page 17.

FOR *KATA*

FOR *KUMITE*

The rules of the *gi*

There are certain standards for a traditional karate *gi* like the one shown below.

The emblem of the school is worn on the left side of the chest.

A traditional *gi* is white and must not have any spots or decoration.

Girls wear a white t-shirt underneath.

One belt

5.9 in (15 cm) long.

Sleeves must not be folded over.

Sleeves should not show the forearm or extend past the wrist.

A
n
k
l
e

Pants should cover 2/3 of the distance between the ankle and the bottom of the knee.

The hem must not be folded over.

Jacket should cover ¾ of the area from the waist to the thigh.

 # The history of the *gi*

The use of a *gi* for karate originated in Okinawa. Initially, the common style for training was a bare upper body with pants and either bare feet or socks. Some wore the jacket from kendo, but there wasn't a specific uniform for karate.

Gichin Funakoshi, considered by many to be the "father of modern day karate," pioneered the use of the *gi*. In 1922, he was invited to travel from his home in Okinawa to demonstrate his style of martial arts in Tokyo. He wore a traditional judo *gi* at the demonstration, and the karate *gi* has been modeled after the judo *gi* ever since.

Photo: Kenwa Mabuni founded the Shito school of karate in the 1930s, which gave rise to four major schools. By that time, the official karate *gi* was in use.

Is a karate *gi* different from a judo *gi*?

Although the karate *gi* originated from the judo *gi*, there are differences. The karate *gi* is made of lighter fabric and is worn more loosely than the judo *gi*. In judo there is much more grappling and throwing, so those parts of the *gi* that are grasped are thicker and more reinforced than the karate *gi*.

Belts and Rank

A karate belt does more than hold the gi *together. It shows rank and degree.*

 ## Rank and degree (*kyu* and *dan*)

As your knowledge of karate grows, you may achieve a new rank (*kyu*). In the United States, this is usually shown by a colored belt or stripes on the belt. There are typically ten ranks. As the student advances, the *kyu* number becomes smaller. After the 1st *kyu* comes 1st *dan*, or first degree black belt. The highest level is 10th *dan* (p. 14). Very high ranking *dan* may wear a red or red-and-white striped belt.

 ## What does it mean to earn a black belt?

Many people think that earning a black belt means that you are a master of martial arts. In Japanese tradition, however, the word for a first degree black belt, *shodan*, means literally "first step." It shows a good understanding of concepts and ability, but recognizes that mastery is never complete. A *shodan* belt represents the beginning of advanced learning, not the end.

Karate skills help develop character even in very young students.

In 2010, Tsuguo Sakumoto reached the rank of 8th *dan*. There are very few who have earned 8th *dan* – out of the 39 who tried in 2010, Tsuguo Sakumoto was the only one who passed.

The significance of belt colors

You can tell competitors' rank from the color of their belt. In simplest terms, a white belt shows *kyu* and the black belt is for *dan*. However, different schools and *dojo* have many other colors, such as orange, yellow, green, purple, and brown.

The black belt that is worn by people who have achieved *dan* is known in Japan as "*kuro obi.*" In the U.S., someone who has achieved *dan* is usually called a "black belt." Telling someone that you have a black belt will make them think twice before attacking you!

Level	Kyu		Dan	
↓ Higher	10TH	White		
	9TH–7TH	Yellow	1ST–8TH dan	Black
	6TH	Green		
	5TH–4TH	Purple		
	3RD–1ST	Brown		

 # Red and blue belts for competition

Belt color does not always indicate rank. In competitions, athletes often wear either a blue or red belt to differentiate themselves. Long ago, karate competitors tied a red or white string over their belt. There was also a time when just a black or white belt was used.

The result of training

Belts are made of colored cloth stitched over a white core. After many years of training, the belt may become white again as the colored fabric wears away. A very worn belt is often considered a sign of prestige.

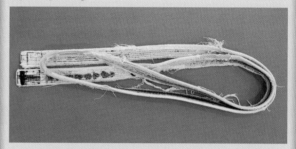

The worn black belt of Ko Matsuhisa, 2007 and 2008 champion of the All Japan Sparring Match

Children with bright orange belts

In this photo, you can see green, purple, brown, and black belts.

The exam

To be awarded an official *dan*, you must pass a test. A panel of judges watches demonstrations of *kata* and sparring ability. There may also be a written test. In order to receive any *dan*, you need to have passed the previous level's test.

For most people, 8th *dan* is the highest rank that can be achieved. There are 9th and 10th *dan*, but these are reserved for those who have devoted their lives to the advancement of karate or made substantial contributions to the art. These special levels of *dan* do not require a test and are called "honorable *dan*" or "recommended *dan*."

DID YOU KNOW?

Where did the degree system of *dan* come from?

In traditional Japanese society, *dan* were awarded to recognize artistic achievement. *Dan* are still awarded for skill in the art of flower arrangement, the tea ceremony, and games of strategy such as go and renju.

Judo was the first martial art to adopt the *dan* system.

Taking the 2010 8th *dan* test

6

How to Wear the *Gi*

*There is a certain protocol to wearing a **gi**. A properly worn **gi** can give its wearer a feeling of confidence and self-respect.*

The parts of the *gi*

Before learning how to wear the *gi*, let's learn the names for the parts of the *gi*.

Collar

Bodice

Where the two sides of the jacket meet.

Sleeve

Cuff

Sleeve

Jacket hem

Crotch

Pant hems

Preparing to compete, with indomitable spirit and a crisp *gi*

How to wear the *gi* properly

The *gi* is worn essentially the same way for both *kata* and *kumite*. Here are the basics of putting on your uniform.

Pants and jacket

1 Put on the pants. Tie any drawstring into a tight bow.

2 Put the jacket on. Bring the right side across; tie the cord.

3 Bring the left side over and do the same thing.

Tying the belt

1 Fold the belt in half. Put the center of the fold on your navel.

Make sure the belt doesn't twist.

Keep it straight on the stomach.

2 With both hands, cross both ends of the belt in the back and bring them to the front.

3 Cross the belt. The belt end in your left hand should go above the one in your right hand.

4 Bring the upper belt end through the belt part that's wrapped around your waist.

Pull this part tightly.

5 Fold the upper belt end down. Push it through the opening you've made and pull it tight.

Don't twist the belt.

For *kumite*, once you've gotten to step 5, you're finished. But for *kata*, there is a little more to learn.

To make the *ohashori*, or fold, put your hand in the place where the two sides of the *gi* meet above the belt. Pull up slightly.

Do the same in back.

Adjust the hem so that the back becomes cylindrical. This will let air flow in.

Pull the front hem to the sides to remove wrinkles.

6 All done!!

For *kumite*

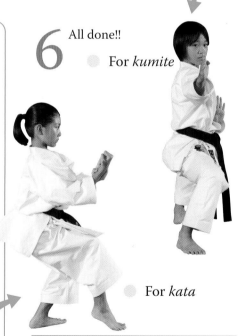

For *kata*

DID YOU KNOW?
Is the karate belt tied the same way as other traditional Japanese clothing?

When you wear the *gi*, you tie the belt in front. For all other traditional Japanese clothing, like the kimono and yukata, both men and women tie it in the back.

7

How to Fold the *Gi*

The gi *is an important part of the karate tradition. By folding it properly, you show respect for the martial arts tradition.*

 ## Correct way of folding

Folding the *gi* properly keeps it looking neat and crisp. There are various ways to fold a karate uniform. This way is one of the most common.

Fold the jacket first

1 Spread the jacket out onto the floor, and make the hems even.

2 Take the shoulder of the jacket and fold it in half. Smooth out any wrinkles.

3 Do the same with the other shoulder. Fold the protruding part back on itself.

4 Fold the pants in half the long way. Tuck in the part that sticks out.

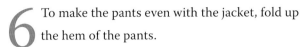

Pants and jacket together

5 Put the pants from step 4 on top of the jacket from step 3.

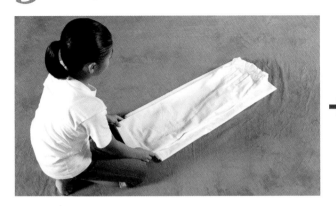

6 To make the pants even with the jacket, fold up the hem of the pants.

7 Taking the jacket and pants together, fold them up one third of the way.

8 Fold them over one more time to finish.

9 Fold the belt.

10 Place the folded belt next to the *gi* from step 8.

DID YOU KNOW?
Can I wash the *gi*?

Usually the *gi* is machine washed after every workout. The *gi* for kata is usually canvas. A new canvas *gi* may be very stiff, but will soften over time with repeated washing.

On the other hand, the *gi* for *kumite* must be lightweight and flexible, so many are made out of synthetic fibers or soft fabrics. The *kumite gi* can also be machine washed.

Making a *gi*

A *gi* must pass through many artisans' hands as it is crafted. This is something we don't normally see, so let's look at how karate *gi* are made.

Jacket and pants

Several steps go into making a jacket and pants that move with the wearer.

1 Purchase fabric

The cloth comes from a factory that makes fabric of the right color and weight needed for the *gi*. The cloth in the photo is about 164 ft (50 m) long.

2 Spread and layer the fabric.

Anti-rolling device. It also holds the ends.

The fabric is spread to a specific length and then folded back on itself multiple times to create several layers. Both ends are then held tightly in a device that keeps the fabric tight and flat. The pattern pieces are drawn on the top layer.

3 Cut the fabric

A special machine is used that can cut through multiple layers of fabric, so many pieces can be cut out at once.

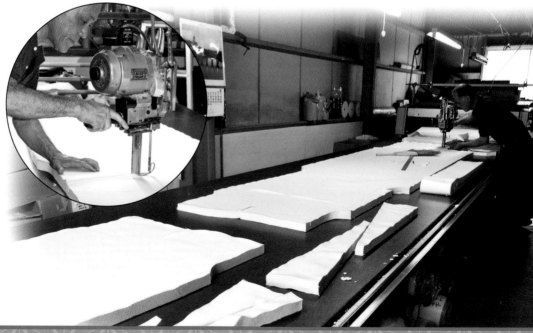

The procedure described here is for making many *gi* at one time. When a *gi* is custom-made, the pieces are cut and sewn by hand.

4 Sewing the cloth

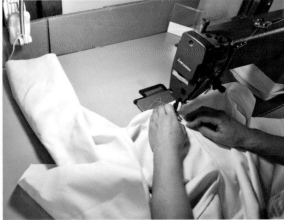

The cloth has been cut.
After this, each piece must be separated and put into a set.

Sometimes the stitching is done completely by machine. A quick check for mistakes and then it is done!

The *gi*'s pants aren't normal pants. They have a gore (also known as a gusset). This allows the pants to flex for high kicks.

5 Adding the embroidery

Once the product is finished, the organization's emblem may be embroidered on the left side of the jacket.

This embroidery is being done completely by machine. Some organizations prefer to sew on an embroidered patch.

Black belt

The belt has a white fabric core with black cotton fabric wrapped over and stitched to it. The type of fabric defines the kind of belt. A belt covered with soft cotton is a *namikuro*. One covered in thicker cotton is a *yohachi*. A satin belt is a *shusu*, and the one that is silk is called *honken*. The belt is either 1.6 in (4 cm) or 1.8 in (4.5 cm) wide.

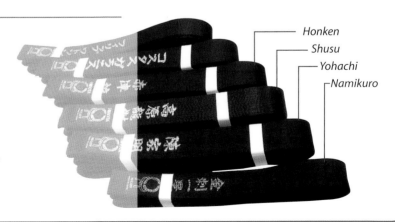

Honken
Shusu
Yohachi
Namikuro

Protective Gear

Special gear is used to prevent injury during sparring and karate competitions. The type of gear varies by type of tournament and the student's age.

 ## The purpose of protective gear

Karate tournaments are not about injuring your opponent. Points are awarded based on accuracy and speed of technique. For that reason, it is usually forbidden to hit or kick an opponent with full force.

However, accidents do happen, and students sometimes get hit. That is why many schools started using protective gear. It not only protects your body from your opponent's blows, but also protects your opponent from getting hurt. Worn properly, the gear reduces the impact on both sides.

 ## Basic protective gear

The basic protective gear protects the hands, head, and chest. In addition, men may wear a cup and women may wear a protective pad on their chest.

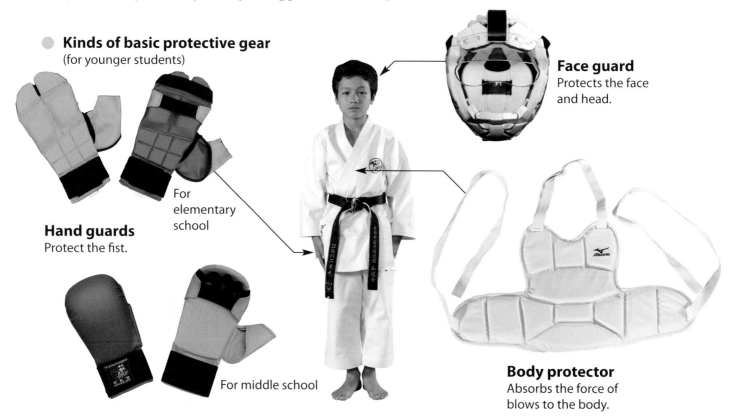

● **Kinds of basic protective gear**
(for younger students)

Hand guards
Protect the fist.

For elementary school

For middle school

Face guard
Protects the face and head.

Body protector
Absorbs the force of blows to the body.

Differences by age and tournament level

The tournaments listed below require more than the basic protective equipment.

● **High school tournament**

Shin guard

Instep guard

Shin guard and instep guard
These protect the top of the foot and shin.

● **International tournament**

Shin and instep guards

A national high school tournament in Japan. Face guards are required.

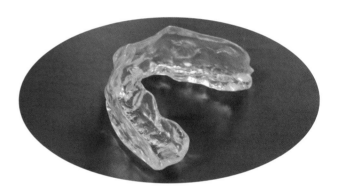

Mouthpiece
This covers the teeth so that you don't bite your own tongue. It may be used in place of a face mask.

● **Cadet (14-15 year olds) World Tournament**

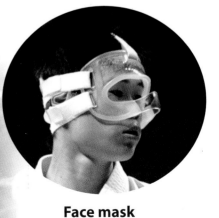

Face mask

Senior World Tournament

The *Dojo*

Karate can be practiced anywhere, but it's usually practiced in a place called the dojo.

 ## Can a gymnasium be a *dojo*?

Ideally, the *dojo* is a space used exclusively for karate, but there are times where a gymnasium is used as a *dojo*.

Dojo were originally attached to temples. As a result, one thing all *dojo* have in common is that a *dojo* is "a place where your mood changes."

During practice, kicks and punches should be controlled so they do not make full contact.

If you or your opponent is not paying attention, one of you could be injured. For that reason, the minute you enter the *dojo*, you must change your frame of mind to one of concentration and respect. If you are mentally focused on practice, then you are less likely to get hurt.

Many *dojo* have small altars or shrines.

You can use the mirrors in a *dojo* to check your movements.

Wood floor

Floor mats are used during competitions (see pages 28–29).

What are the *dojo kun* (rules)?

Many *dojo* hang up their rules. The rules are principles to be followed while studying karate. Since they are written concisely, many *dojo* post them in highly visible places. There are also many who sit in *seiza* before practice and recite the rules.

Example of rules
- **Courtesy**
- **Integrity**
- **Perseverance**
- **Self-control**
- **Indomitable spirit**

Dojo rules posted in a Japanese *dojo*.

DOJO KUN

HITOTSU

JINKAKU KANSEI NI TSUTOMURO KOTO

MAKOTO NO MICHI O MAMORU KOTO

DORYOKU NO SEISHIN O YASHINAU KOTO

REIGI O OMONZURU KOTO

KEKKI NO YU O IMASHIMURU KOTO

Dojo rules in Miami, Florida, written in transliterated Japanese

DID YOU KNOW?
What is Japan's biggest *dojo*?

Japan's biggest *dojo* is the Nippon Budokan. The main site and arena are 1.6 square miles (2,513m^2).

The Nippon Budokan hosts domestic and international music concerts and many other events. However, as the name suggests, it was originally built as a place for young people to study martial arts like kendo and judo. It was completed in 1964, the same year that judo became an Olympic sport. Even now, the Nippon Budokan hosts most of the important martial arts tournaments and championships in Japan.

This is the Nippon Budokan's triangular roof. You can see the buildings of Tokyo in the background.

The 2008 opening ceremony for the World Karate Championships, hosted at the Nippon Budokan

Karate across the globe

Karate has now spread all over the world. Many countries have *dojo*. Let's look at some different *dojo* and students during practice.

● China

China's national team, shown below and to the left, has been getting stronger. The red letters are the *dojo kun*, or rules of conduct. In the front, rule #3 is written. Rule #5 is posted in back (see p. 25).

● Dominican Republic

A *dojo* in the Dominican Republic. Dominicans are strong in *kata*. In 2009, a Dominican girl won 2nd place in *kata* in a world tournament.

● Turkey

In 2008, the male team won the *kumite* section during the World Karate Championships. Turkey also won two individual medals.

● Czech Republic

Here, members of a Czech *dojo* listen to a visiting Japanese instructor. When a high-ranking visiting instructor comes, it is called *gasshuku*, or warrior training.

● Spain

This picture shows Spain's national team on a trip to train in China. Traveling to study in another *dojo* is called *degeiko*. Spain is one of the most competitive countries and has won many trophies.

●USA

This photo is of a group of students doing morning practice in Miami, Florida. Miami has very warm weather year round, so many schools hold practice on the beach.

Competition Arena

Training usually takes place on a padded mat or a wooden floor. Competitions always take place on a regulation mat, called the competition grounds or arena.

Rules of the competition arena

Regulations state that all karate competition, whether *kata* or *kumite*, must take place on a safe, flat surface. For *kumite*, the competition area is as seen in the picture below, 26.3 ft (8m) on each side. This area is called *jonai*, or in bounds. The 3.3 ft (1 m) border around the outside is called *jogai*, or out of bounds. The background color of the mat is white for domestic competition and blue for international tournaments. The border line may be different colors depending on whether it is a regional or international competition.

A mat on the ground helps to prevent injuries.

Here you can clearly see where the out of bounds line (*jogai*) is.

1 m

6 m

1 m

8 m

8 m

The mat

The karate mat is made of foam covered with vinyl. It is made to absorb impacts without slipping around on the floor.

The packed crowd at an international competition in Germany shows how popular karate is.

The Junior Cadet (14-17 years old) competition in Morocco. Look how the *tatami* are all lined up.

What is the *tatami* in karate?

The straw mat that is used in Japanese-style rooms is called *tatami* all over the world. For karate training the floor is wood, and for competition it's a mat. There isn't anything that is actually a straw mat, or *tatami*, but at international competitions each court is called *tatami*.

International arena. "*Tatami* 2" means the same thing as "Court 2."

INDEX

GLOSSARY

Japanese Transliteration	Pronunciation	Meaning
Budo	*Boo-doe*	Martial arts
Degeiko	*Deh-gey-ko*	Going to another dojo to train
Dogi	*Doe-gee (hard g)*	Uniform for kata and kumite
Dojo	*Doe-joe*	Training room
Gasshuku	*Gah-shoo-koo*	Going to another dojo to train
Gi	*Gee (hard g)*	Uniform
Jogai	*Joe-gai (a like father)*	Out of bounds
Jonai	*Joe-nai*	In bounds
Honken	*Hohn-ken*	Silk belt
Karate-do	*Kah-rah-teh-doe*	Way of karate
Kata	*Kah-tah*	Form, sequence of movements
Kumite	*Koo-mee-tay*	Sparring
Namikuro	*Nah-me-koo-roe*	Soft cotton belt
Rei	*Ray*	Bow(ing)
Reisetsu	*Ray-seh-tsoo*	Etiquette
Ritsurei	*Rit-su-ray*	Standing bow
Setsu	*Seh-tsoo*	Principle
Seiza	*Say-za*	Kneel(ing)
Shusu	*Shoo-soo*	Satin belt
Tatami	*Tah-tah-mee*	Floor mat
Yohachi	*Yo-hah-chee*	Hard cotton belt
Zarei	*Zah-ray*	Sitting Bow

WEBSITES

Karate World:
http://www.karatedo.co.jp/index3.htm

World Karate Federation:
http://www.wkf.net/index.php

Japan Karatedo Federation:
http://www.karatedo.co.jp/jkf/jkf-eng/e_index.htm

This edition published in 2013 by The Oliver Press, Inc.
Charlotte Square
5707 West 36th Street
Minneapolis, MN 55416-2510

KARATE MADE SIMPLE: ETIQUETTE, EQUIPMENT, AND THE DOJO

Original Japanese title: KIHON WO KIWAMERU! KARATEDO: REI/KARATEGI/DOJO
(Mastering the Basics! Karatedo: Etiquette, Uniform, and Training Center)
© Champ Co., Ltd., 2011
All rights reserved.
Original Japanese edition published in 2011 by Champ Co., Ltd.
English translation rights with Imajinsha Co., Ltd. through Japan UNI Agency, Inc., Tokyo

Library of Congress Cataloging-in-Publication Data

Nakashima, Maiko.
Karate made simple 1 : etiquette, equipment and the dojo / Maiko Nakashima with the Japan Karate Federation.
    p. cm. -- (Karate made simple)
Includes bibliographical references and index.
ISBN 978-1-934545-17-1
1. Karate--Juvenile literature. I. Title.
GV1114.3.N35 2012
796.815'3--dc23
                          2012033028

Text: Maiko Nakashima with the Japan Karate Federation
Translation: Chiaki Hasegawa and Goldie Gibbs
U.S. editing: April Stern
U.S. production: Clay Schotzko

Picture Credits:
All images courtesy of Champ Co., Ltd. and Imajinsha Co., Ltd.

ISBN: 978-1-934545-17-1
Printed in the United States of America
17 16 15 14 13   8 7 6 5 4 3 2 1